Strong Sisters of Strength Ministries presents

MARRIAGE
IN REVIEW

IT ALL STARTS WITH YOU

DR. CECILIA WILSON SMITH

XULON PRESS

Xulon Press
2301 Lucien Way #415
Maitland, FL 32751
407.339.4217
www.xulonpress.com

Paperback ISBN-13: 978-1-6628-2209-4

Marriage In Review

Dedication

This book is dedicated to my dear family I was born with, as well as my family at Global Oved Dei Seminary and University, my Mount Olive Baptist Church family, and ALL my Strong Sisters of Strength. I also dedicate this book to all the people who have a sincere desire to be married and truly dedicated to becoming personally responsible for truly loving their spouse the way God loves each of us.

Table of Contents

Introduction

I am honored to be chosen to complete this marriage book assignment. My sincere prayer is that the contents of this book will empower someone to become a better spouse. I pray this teaching will be the answer to someone's prayer.

Through my own marriage experience, God has allowed me to see marriage the way He sees it. Genesis 2:24 (NKJV) says, "Therefore, a man shall leave his father and mother and be joined to his wife, and they shall become one flesh." Thus, I have learned to think twice about how I treat my flesh as well as my marriage. Just as my flesh is a part of me, so is my marriage. I had made my first marriage about me. I felt it was time for me to marry, so I married. However, my current marriage is about God, and I am simply a willing vessel in His Story. I am most grateful to God for allowing me a second opportunity to follow His marital instructions clearly in His Word, in which He truly has a blueprint for marriage. It is our choice to follow His plan or not.

Prayerfully, my findings will be instrumental in helping another willing participant who really desires to follow God's plan for marriage. I have learned that until I cherished my relationship with God, I was not able to cherish my relationship with my husband. I could close the book with that thought, but I will not. I have more to share with you.

Chapter 1
Marriage Starts with You

I have learned that it is easier to hold a spouse accountable than to hold yourself accountable for actions that take place in a marriage. Your marriage starts with you. The answers to the following questions will help your marriage thrive.

Questions to Ponder:

A GOOGLE search will disclose that the word "ponder" is defined as "to think about (something) carefully, especially before making a decision or reaching a conclusion."

Before you say "I do," answer the following questions. If the answer is just "yes" or "no," take some time to explain your answer more fully.

1. How do I define marriage?

_____

_____

2. Why do I think I am ready to be married?

_____

_____

3. Do I know who and whose I am?

_____

_____

4. Do I like who I am?

_____

_____

5. Do I live a balanced Christian life?

_____

_____

6. Do I suffer from childhood scars or trauma?

_____

_____

7. Do I suffer from forgiveness issues?

_____

_____

8. Women: Was my father a Christian gentleman?
    Was he my knight in shining armor?

_____

_____

9. Men: Was your mom a Super Woman? Did she
    do it ALL????

_____

_____

10. Do I know what I need from a spouse?

_____

_____

11. Do I know what I have to offer a spouse?

_____

_____

12. Why do I want to be married?

_____

_____

Challenge: Rather than blame my spouse for what happens, I will hold myself accountable for what happens in my marriage.

Scriptures to Memorize:

"But seek first the kingdom of God and His righteousness, and all these things shall be added to you." – Matthew 6:33 (NKJV)

"For what profit is it to a man if he gains the whole world, and loses his own soul? Or what will a man give in exchange for his soul?" – Matthew 16:26 (NKJV)

Chapter 2
Marriage Is Asking the Real Questions

What questions do you ask potential mates? I have learned most people dating to marry have no idea how important premarital conversations are to a healthy relationship that could lead to marriage. I have also noticed most people try really hard to make an amazing first impression on their potential mate; therefore, they practice only asking questions that are extremely positive to ensure a positive response from their date, so the real marital questions do not come up in the conversation.

Most times, neither person wants to be offensive or hurtful. While being respectful is necessary when engaging in any encounter, it is still important to <u>ask</u>

<u>the real questions</u>. The answers to these questions could potentially help you decide if you are spending time with the mate who is right for you. These questions are especially helpful if you are truly considering spending the rest of your lives together in the same house. Not only is it important to ask the right questions, but it is even more important to await an answer to the questions.

Here are some questions to consider asking your potential spouse:

* What is your legal name on your birth certificate?
* Who are your parents?
* What aspect of your childhood is most important to you?
* When did you accept Jesus as your personal Lord and Savior?
* What ministry do you serve in at your church and why?
* What weekly Bible study do you attend?
* What is your greatest accomplishment in life?
* What has been your greatest disappointment?
* What is your five-year plan?

+ Have you ever been or do you want to be married with children?

In the space below, write down some additional questions you may want to ask:

_____

_____

_____

_____

_____

Scriptures to Memorize:

"Death and life are in the power of the tongue, And those who love it will eat its fruit. He who finds a wife finds a good thing, And obtains favor from the LORD." – Proverbs 18:21-22 (NKJV)

"A new commandment I give to you, that you love one another; as I have loved you, that you also love one another. By this all will know that you are My disciples, if you have love for one another." – John 13:34-35 (NKJV)

Chapter 3
Marriage is Fasting for Spiritual Breakthrough

Does fasting for spiritual breakthrough ever occur to you as a necessary, essential, recurring action? Fasting involves sacrificing something you like so that you can gain something you want from God.

Sometimes your emotions can be so noisy that you can't hear Holy Spirit speaking to you. When you are talking too much, you can't hear His still, small voice. Your desires can be so loud that they can distract you from what God has for you. Fasting facilitates spiritual discipline, allowing you to focus on what Holy Spirit is saying to you. In my own life, fasting has proven to be very instrumental in my hearing from

Holy Spirit. The topic of marriage can be so complicated, and it is easy to miss what is important among all the rhetoric. Fasting allows you to clearly hear what Holy Spirit is saying to you about a potential mate or your current spouse, and it also truly allows you to focus on God rather than your mate. Once you can clearly hear from God, listening to your mate will become much easier.

Challenge: For forty days, fast and pray for marital insight and breakthrough to determine your next move before you say "I do." Let Holy Spirit allow you to determine what your fast will look like. Begin to pray mightily and journal what Holy Spirit says to you before, during, and after your forty days. Before you talk yourself out of it, just try fasting and praying. Stop right now and pray. After you pray, sit a while and listen. Be still and listen. Then, use the following lines to write down what comes to your mind as you sit and think for 30 minutes. (6 lines)

Scriptures to Memorize:

"When you fast, do not look somber as the hypocrites do, for they disfigure their faces to show others they are fasting. Truly I tell you, they have received their reward in full. – Matthew 6:16

"However, this kind does not go out except by prayer and fasting." – Matthew 17:21

Chapter 4
Marriage Is Following the Plan God Has for You

I n every area of your life, including your mar-riage, you must pray for guidance. As God's child, please know He loves you dearly. He becomes your Father when you accept His gift of His Son and become indwelled by the Holy Spirit. God created you in His own image. Once you truly comprehend the love God has for you, you will never settle for anything from a man or woman that is less than what He wants for you.

God would never lead you where you shouldn't be. Most women assume they should be married with two kids and live happily ever after. Please don't assume. Just ask your Heavenly Father for His plan for your life. Please pray for wisdom. If you are wise enough to follow God's plan, everything else will fall into place. However, most people are following their own plan and doing what is right in their own eyes. If you do this, your consequences can be difficult at best. Have you ever realized you made a mistake? If so, have you proceeded to convince everyone around you that you actually made the right choice? Have you considered how much time you've wasted refusing to admit your mistake? The sooner you admit fault, the quicker you can move on. Praying for guidance will save you a lot of time and energy. Always seek Godly counsel, and ask God who to go to in order to seek Godly guidance; don't assume you know, for looks can be extremely deceiving. Your thoughts may not be God's thoughts, and your plan may not be God's plan. Who do you think knows best? God knows best. Your feelings are faulty.

Questions to Ponder:

1. Is Marriage God's plan for me in this season?

_____

_____

2. Am I ready to follow God's plan for my life?

_____

_____

Scriptures to Memorize:

"For I know the thoughts that I think toward you, says the LORD, thoughts of peace and not of evil, to give you a future and a hope." – Jeremiah 29:11 (NKJV)

"Jesus grew in wisdom and in stature and in favor with God and all the people." – Luke 2:52 (NLT) (Memorize this verse with your name in it.)

"If any of you lacks wisdom, let him ask of God, who gives to all liberally and without reproach, and it will be given to him." – James 1:5 (NKJV)

Chapter 5
Marriage Is a Commitment to God

A commitment is an obligation to do something, and a successful marriage is a true <u>commitment of excellence</u>. You are either committed to mediocrity or committed to greatness; either way, you are committed. Every day, you decide what your commitment level is in your marriage. The daily question you must ask yourself is, do you want to be committed to your marriage? You decide what your commitment looks like in your marital relationship each day.

Question to Ponder:

What and who am I committed to?

_____

_____

Scripture to Memorize:

"And Adam said: 'This is now bone of my bones and flesh of my flesh; she shall be called Woman, because she was taken out of Man.' Therefore a man shall leave his father and mother and be joined to his wife, and they shall become one flesh.' – Genesis 2:23-24

Chapter 6

Marriage Is Loving Your Spouse the Way God Loves You

S o many people do not believe they are loved by our Heavenly Father God. So many people continue to relive every mistake they ever made. God loves us so much he allows us the free will to do what we desire. He lovingly allows us to choose each day whom we will serve. He allows us the free will to do as we please. He continues to cover us with his Grace, Mercy and protection. He continues to still wake us up and allow us to move freely about this earth. I am not sure why we would not choose to love our spouse as God so freely loves us.

The longer I live, the more I realize just how much God loves me. John 3:16 (NIV) says, "For God so loved the world that he gave his one and only Son, that whoever believes in him shall not perish but have eternal life."

Questions to Ponder:

1. Do I have the capacity to love my spouse the way the Lord loves me? (Capacity is the ability or capability to do something.)

\
\

2. Do I want to love my spouse the way the Lord loves me? The Lord loves us so much He sent His only begotten Son (sacrifice).

\
\

3. How much am I willing to sacrifice for my marriage? (Sacrifice is the act of giving up something you want.)

\
\

Scripture to Memorize:

"Give thanks to the Lord, for he is good! His faithful love endures forever." – 1 Chronicles 16:34 (NLT)

Chapter 7
Marriage Is Filtering the Words That Come out of Your Mouth

Your words dictate what actions you will take. Thus, you must learn to watch your words before you speak. Always think before you speak. Asking yourself if what you are about to say to your spouse is helpful will enhance your marriage.

Questions to Ponder:

1. Am I committed to watching the words I say to my spouse?

_____

_____

2. Am I interested in how my spouse feels about what I say to him/her?

_____

_____

3. Do I know I have the ability to think before I speak?

_____

_____

Questions to consider before you speak to your spouse:

+ Why do I need to say this?
+ When do I need to say this?
+ How do I need to say this?
+ Remember, whatever I say matters...

Scripture to Memorize:

"Death and life are in the power of the tongue, And those who love it will eat its fruit." – Proverbs 18:21

Chapter 8
Marriage Is Work

M aintaining a healthy marriage takes effort and intentionality. I call it work. Work is activity involved in achieving a result. Making a daily effort to intentionally sustain a healthy marriage is paramount to your marital covenant.

Questions to Ponder:

1. How can I pray for my marriage today?

_____

_____

2. How do I support my marriage?

_____

_____

3. How do I focus on being the best spouse I can be?

_____

_____

Scripture to Memorize:

"He who finds a wife finds a good thing, And obtains favor from the LORD." – Proverbs 18:22 (NKJV)

Chapter 9
Marriage Is Learning to Share Life

In the midst of the wedding-planning process, few couples really envision living in the same house, where they will be sharing the same space all day, every day. Learning to live daily with a spouse is not easy. It sometimes takes a lifetime to adjust to sharing your life.

Questions to Ponder:

1. Do I want to share my life?

_____

_____

2. Why do I want to share my life?

_____

_____

Scripture to Memorize:

"Therefore, a man shall leave his father and mother
and be joined to his wife, and they shall become one
flesh." – Genesis 2:24 (NKJV)

Chapter 10
Marriage is an Incredible Experience with Your Mate Approved by God

Some people marry their best friend. Some people marry the love of their life. Some people marry their soul mate. However, most folks fail to ask for God's approval on their chosen mate. Thank God for free will, yet we obviously should seek wise counsel to wisely choose the one person with whom we will spend the rest of our lives. Marriage can be an incredible experience with the right mate approved by God.

Questions to Ponder:

1. How much time do I invest in preparing to get married?

_____

_____

2. How much time do I have to invest in choosing the right mate?

_____

_____

3. How much time do I have to invest in my marriage?

_____

_____

Scriptures to Memorize:

"But true wisdom and power are found in God; counsel and understanding are his." – Job 12:13 (NLT)

"Trust in the LORD with all your heart, And lean not on your own understanding; In all your ways acknowledge Him, And He shall direct your paths." – Proverbs 3:5-6 (NKJV)

Please know your marriage will struggle mightily if you do not pray mightily. No prayer, no marriage. Occasional Prayer, occasional marriage. Do consider intentionally praying for your marriage before and during your marriage. Start and end each day with Prayer. Intentionally pray each day for your marriage. I have learned to intentionally pray each day for all marriages. Imagine what would happen f we all prayed daily for marriages. How many marriages would be saved from divorce court? Start today praying for your marriage as well as ALL marriages.

Marriage Prayers:

Prayer for Singles:

> Dear God,
>
> I pray that as I come together to join my spouse in holy matrimony, I will take my marital covenant (vow) and my responsibilities extremely seriously. Lord, as

committed I am to serving you, I am just as committed to serving my spouse.

In the name of Jesus, I pray.
Amen.

Prayer for the Married:

Dear God,

I pray each day that I will be true to my spouse and to You. May I never forget that you joined us together for a purpose and for a kingdom assignment.

In the name of Jesus, I pray.
Amen.

Prayer for Marriages:

Dear God,

I pray that all husbands will love their wives as Christ loves the Church and gave Himself for her (Eph. 5:25). I pray that wives will love their husbands (Titus 2:4).

Lord, may You be the center of all marriages so that You will bless and highly favor each couple's lives. May You be honored through each Christian marriage, a representation of Christ and His Bride.

And may each one of us as Christians be worthy of our Lord Jesus, as we look forward to the day when we will be united with Him.

In the name of Jesus, I pray.
Amen.

Homework:

Write your own Marriage Prayer:

_____

_____

_____

_____

_____

_____

Closing Thoughts

Now, you've read my thoughts on marriage, and you should seriously consider sharing your own thoughts. You have thoughts and opinions about marriage too. Allow Holy Spirit to guide you in all truth. If you need more support, don't hesitate to reach out to me. I've likely been where you are trying to go. I'm honored to have been a conduit for Holy Spirit to speak to you about marriage. Please pray mightily that the Lord will continue to connect me to His people who need His help. I'm a very willing vessel He's continuing to use.

Sincerely yours,
Dr. Cecilia W. Smith
Founder & CEO
of Strong Sisters of Strength Ministries, Inc.

#AWillingVessel
#AWalkingPrayer